CAREERS AS A
Cyberterrorism Expert

JASON PORTERFIELD

ROSEN
PUBLISHING

Published in 2011 by The Rosen Publishing Group, Inc.
29 East 21st Street, New York, NY 10010

Library of Congress Cataloging-in-Publication Data

Porterfield, Jason.
Careers as a cyberterrorism expert / Jason Porterfield.—1st ed.
    p. cm.—(Careers in computer technology)
Includes bibliographical references and index.
ISBN 978-1-4488-1316-2 (library binding)
1. Cyberterrorism. 2. Electronic data processing—Vocational guidance.
3. Computer science—Vocational guidance. I. Title.
HV6773.P67 2010
363.325'9004—dc22

2010008929

Manufactured in the United States of America

CPSIA Compliance Information: Batch #W11YA: For further information, contact Rosen Publishing, New York, New York, at 1-800-
237-9932.

On the cover: Cybersoldiers update antivirus software designed to fend off
cyber attacks for air force units in Louisiana.

Contents

Cyberterrorism is a criminal practice that has greatly evolved due to the world's increasing reliance on computers and information technology. In recent years, cyberterrorism has grown from a vague concept to a frightening reality. Cyberterrorists work to undermine the security of governments, disrupt communications, and steal classified and sensitive information by breaking into computer networks. The threat of cyberterrorism looms large over a world in which networks are used for storing public records, managing vital services, facilitating communication, and transferring money. The threat has grown rapidly because cyberterrorists have become more knowledgeable about getting around security measures.

The new and exciting field of cyberterrorism expert, or cybersoldier, has emerged to meet the challenge posed by cyberterrorists. Cybersoldiers are men and women with backgrounds in computers. Many have received training from the military or from law enforcement or intelligence agencies. They have developed the skills needed to launch counterattacks against cyberterrorists on the digital plane.

Training for cybersoldiers is undertaken mostly through military or federal agencies. Before arriving at these training programs, cybersoldiers often receive an education in computer science, information technology, or computer engineering. Many have backgrounds in network security and understand how some basic operations, such as simple computer hacks, are carried out.

They have the creativity needed to instantly adapt to threats on a network and cloak their presence on an enemy's network. Cybersoldiers must also have the ability to learn new techniques for defeating security measures and the tenacity to maintain a prolonged attack against a cyberterrorist network. Cybersoldiers should have strong knowledge of how computer networks work. Problem-solving skills and curiosity are also useful in the field.

Cyberterrorism experts for the United States operate around the world as part of the nation's military forces. They work out of offices in major cities for intelligence agencies. Some work for private companies with government contracts. In the future, cybersoldiers may be employed to protect private companies. As the threat of cyberterrorism increases, the need for cybersoldiers will grow.

CHAPTER 1

What Is Cyberterrorism?

The nature of warfare is constantly changing. Nations are frequently updating the technology used by their armed forces. In turn, this new technology calls for tactics to be regularly updated in response to demands on the battlefield. Military strategists look for weaknesses in their enemies and strike when they find a vulnerability.

In the twenty-first century, a nation's computer systems and networks are among those vulnerabilities. In the United States, much of the population is connected to the Internet at home, work, or school. People have come to rely on computers and mobile electronic devices such as smartphones for communication and commerce.

The military, government, and businesses are also increasingly reliant on computer networks. In recent years, the military's use of computer networks and information systems has increased rapidly. Every function of the military, from operations logistics to intelligence work to command and control, uses computer networks and relies to some extent on the electronic transfer of information. The government relies on networks for storing vast amounts of data, including vital personal records and information related to the nation's defense. Businesses and corporations send information over networks on everything from scheduling to financial transactions.

The Department of Homeland Security often practices by conducting mock cyber attacks. For example, the "Cyber Storm" simulation enacts a mock cyber raid by antiglobalization activists.

This reliance on information networks makes them a tantalizing target to the nation's enemies, who may see an underprotected network as a strategic place to strike a blow. Coordinated attacks against computer networks are often called cyberterrorism, and the use of such attacks to disrupt another nation's operations is often referred to as cyber warfare.

CYBERTERRORISTS

Cyberterrorists are usually individuals who are extremely knowledgeable in how information networks are interconnected and how information is transferred through networks. Many are self-taught computer hackers, and they trade information on how to exploit network vulnerabilities. They are skilled in circumventing network security protocols and finding back doors into otherwise secure networks.

Cyberterrorists can do a great deal of damage by exploiting network weaknesses. Their attacks can be relatively small in scale and carried out to retrieve some vital piece of information, or they can be large-scale assaults by multiple cyberterrorists who attack a network in waves in hopes of making it crash. By exploiting networks, they could crash phone systems, disrupt transportation schedules, or even wipe out financial information.

Cyberterrorists seek to disrupt their perceived enemies. They may work independently of known terrorist groups or as part of such organizations. In some cases, nations have been accused of cyberterrorism. In one recent high-profile case, a three-week-long cyber attack was carried out against the nation of Estonia's Web sites. The attacks threatened to cripple the high-tech nation, where the Internet is routinely used for services ranging from voting to paying for parking.

The scale of the attack was so massive that the Estonian government was forced to sacrifice sites that it deemed less vital in order to protect others. In the heaviest day of the attack, the network of the nation's largest bank's was so overwhelmed that it was forced to shut down for more than an hour. The Estonian government charged that the attack had come from Russia, its longtime antagonist, although neither the Russian government nor its military could be linked to the attack. Russia denied involvement.

AWAKENING AWARENESS

The Estonian case helped awaken the world to the potential threat posed by cyberterrorists. Nations saw that they needed to develop tactics that could be used to defend themselves against such threats. Along with a growing awareness of the need for a high-quality cybersecurity workforce capable of thwarting such attacks, governments also determined that they needed to focus on developing strategies for using cyber warfare methods to strike back against cyberterrorists.

The U.S. military, however, had begun laying the groundwork for its own cyber warfare operations in the 1990s. In January

Lieutenant Colonel Ilmar Tamm of Estonia's Cooperative Cyber Defence Centre of Excellence speaks at a news conference. The Estonian cyber attacks brought global attention to the need for effective cyber defense.

1995, the U.S. secretary of defense established the Information Warfare Executive Board. The board was given the task of developing information warfare goals. Later that year, a policy paper called the Presidential Decision Directive 39 set the nation's policies concerning the threat of terrorism. That document also contained details relating to information warfare.

In 1996, the government established the President's Commission on Critical Infrastructure Protection, with the goal of assessing physical and cyber threats to critical infrastructure and developing strategies to defend against such attacks. At the same time, the Infrastructure Protection Task Force was created to increase the government's coordination of infrastructure protection. In 1998, these two agencies were followed by the National Infrastructure Protection Center, located at the FBI's and U.S. Department of Commerce's Critical Infrastructure Assurance Office. A third project called the Federal Intrusion Detection Network was put into place that year to protect government and key private sector computer nodes though system and network monitoring.

In 2000, the U.S. government issued its National Plan for Information Systems Protection. The plan described the country's new dependencies on information systems and the threats posed to these systems. The document proposed partnerships between the public and private sectors and the establishment of training programs to develop cyber defense capabilities. In 2002, the President's Critical Infrastructure Protection Board published a report called the "National Strategy to Secure Cyberspace," while Congress's Joint Economic Committee released a document called "Security in the Information Age" describing a range of perspectives on protecting infrastructure.

CYBER DEFENSE IN SCHOOLS

Cyberterrorism is such a major threat that there are nationwide campaigns dedicated to teaching cyberterrorism defense in schools. High-level organizations are working to attract tech professionals to combat cyber threats.

Competitions such as the Collegiate Cyber Defense Competition and the US Cyber Challenge have attracted a number of high school and college students. Even the defense contractor Boeing Corporation has gotten involved by hiring contestants to defend its networks, which are targets for spies.

In addition to the competition, colleges and universities are investing in cybersecurity training. Programs such as CyberWatch, a two-year training program offered by a collection of mid-Atlantic colleges, promote cybersecurity training.

At the grade-school level, two Maryland counties offer "information assurance" as a career track for K–12 students in an effort to raise cybersecurity awareness among young people who are involved in social media.

Infrastructure that could prove vulnerable to cyber warfare includes information and communication systems, energy production and distribution systems, physical distribution systems such as railroads and highways, banking and finance institutions, and vital human services such as emergency services. Much of this information infrastructure is interconnected, and the impact of a cyberterrorist attack shutting down one sector would be difficult to gauge. Two sectors, energy and information and communication, are necessary for the operation of the others, and an attack against one of the two could have the widest effect.

President Barack Obama greets Cybersecurity Coordinator Howard Schmidt shortly after appointing him to the position. Schmidt has an extensive background in security and computer forensics.

SHIFTING STRATEGY

In the past, America's focus was on defending against such attacks by developing stronger firewalls and network security procedures. However, that strategy recently shifted. In January 2010, Pentagon officials met to stage a simulated cyber attack against the nation's power grids, its financial networks, and its communication systems.

The results of the exercise showed that in such situations the attackers would have the advantages of stealth and anonymity, while their actions would be completely unpredictable.

The officials could not pinpoint the origin of the simulated attack and lacked the legal authority to respond, since it could not be determined whether the simulated attack was an act of vandalism, an attempted commercial theft, or an effort to cripple the nation by a foreign power. The results of the simulation suggested that in cases of cyber warfare, defensive strategies may not be enough.

The question of how to react to cyberterrorism has extended to other parts of the government. The National Security Agency (NSA) secretly sifts through overseas computer networks in search of evidence of pending cyber attacks. Officials at the agency have questioned whether knowledge of a pending cyber attack would give them the justification to launch a preemptive cyber attack against cyberterrorists in order to cripple their capabilities.

In December 2009, President Barack Obama named Howard Schmidt the nation's first cybersecurity coordinator. The coordinator's job calls for him to direct branches of the military and government as they work to ward off cyber attacks from terrorists, governments, hackers, criminal organizations, and others who want to shut down key networks. The government's increased focus on cybersecurity means more job opportunities in the field of network security, but it also means that more opportunities are opening up for cybersoldiers.

CYBERSOLDIERS

The U.S. government has not specified whether it would make preemptive cyber attacks against an enemy if it perceived a threat. However, the military has engaged in these tactics in the past. During the nation's military action in Kosovo in 1998, hackers from the United States hacked into the Serbian air defense system and tricked Serbian air traffic controllers so that U.S. and NATO planes could bomb targets with few casualties.

The ability to hack into a complex system is just one quality that a cybersoldier must possess. In many cases, the work performed by a cybersoldier will likely be very similar to the work done by a cyberterrorist. The difference would be that cybersoldiers would be racing against cyberterrorists in order to prevent an attack.

Cybersoldiers must have a deep knowledge of how computer systems and networks function. As the term is still relatively new and largely undefined, cybersoldiers could find themselves performing tasks ranging from hacking into systems to data mining. They should be able to reverse engineer software. In the past, many of these people would have been largely self-taught. Today, formalized education programs are being built to teach the skills needed by cybersoldiers. These programs can be found at the public university level, within branches of the military or government, and at private companies that specialize in network security.

Today's cybersoldiers learn the basics of information security, knowledge that can help them get around firewalls and other security measures. They learn about computer forensics, which involves investigating computer hardware and storage devices in order to trace a cyber attack to its source. Cybersoldiers must also learn espionage techniques so that they can enter networks and locate valuable information without being discovered and traced.

I n the course of their work, cybersoldiers must be prepared to perform some of the same operations as cyberterrorists. In some ways, the line between the two is fine, and cybersoldiers may find themselves carrying out operations that would be considered cyberterrorism if they were directed against the United States. They must remember that their actions are an important part of national security and that they are providing a valuable service to the nation by disrupting cyberterror attacks before they can be carried out.

TERRORISTS AND THE INTERNET

The first computer networks were created by the U.S. military during the 1960s as a way of providing rapid and secure communications in the event of a catastrophe. Networks later became part of academic and business cultures, as universities and research centers connected through networks and industries such as banking and transportation set up their own computer networks. During the late 1980s and early 1990s, a worldwide research and funding effort led to the development and commercialization of a worldwide network called the Internet.

Today, an estimated one-quarter of the world's population uses the Internet for communication, research, banking, shopping, and numerous other purposes scarcely imagined when the first networks were developed. People around the world who share common interests can now communicate with ease using ever-adapting programs and interfaces.

Unfortunately, the Internet also serves as an ideal way for terrorists to communicate. Terrorist leaders can use the Internet to easily connect with their followers to spread propaganda and instructions. They also use it to launch psychological scare campaigns and communicate with other terrorist groups and sympathetic organizations.

The Internet has a number of advantages for modern terrorism: It is decentralized, it cannot be easily controlled or restricted, it isn't censored, and it allows access to virtually

Terrorist groups often use the Internet to keep their followers in touch and spread propaganda, such as this video of Al Qaeda chief Osama bin Laden, which appeared in 2007.

anyone who wants to connect. The Internet is an easy and convenient tool for terrorists to use in making threats and spreading fear. They can set up Web sites, send e-mail, upload and download information, and use forums such as chat rooms, e-groups, online magazines, and message boards. The Internet provides them with the anonymity needed to operate in social environments that may be opposed to their beliefs and practices.

The Internet also provides terrorists with a low-risk means of striking out at their perceived enemies. By spreading threats and propaganda, they can attempt to sway public opinion to their cause. By using the Internet to steal information or disable a computer network, terrorists can strike a blow and then fade back into anonymity.

EQUIPMENT DISRUPTION

One of the most vital operations for a cybersoldier is the disruption of an enemy's equipment. Cyberterrorists have long attempted to hack into government networks and attack infrastructure by disrupting equipment. A disruption could consist of anything from scrambling data to installing programs meant to completely shut the network down.

A carefully planned disruption could cause havoc for an enemy. Targets for disruption can include air traffic control equipment, banking systems, or military communications. Cybersoldiers engaged in activities against terrorists would likely attempt to target the terrorists' computer hardware as a preemptive attack. They may also go after conventional terrorists in an attempt to disable their communications systems before an attack can be launched.

A well-coordinated cyber attack against a sensitive computer network, such as one used by air traffic controllers, could cause widespread service disruptions and put lives at risk.

Cybersoldiers performing these tasks would have to know how to hack into an enemy's computer systems. They would also need a basic understanding of the system being targeted and knowledge of its specific weak points. They also would have to be prepared to cover their tracks after carrying out the operation and even redirect any suspicion to another entity.

CYBER ESPIONAGE

Cyber espionage is the act of gathering secrets without the permission of the holder. Cyberterrorists can victimize individuals, corporations, governments, and the military through cyber espionage. Practitioners exploit the Internet, networks, and personal computers using a variety of techniques. They may use software designed to "crack" passwords or check computers and networks for vulnerabilities. Once inside, they use additional programs to uncover sensitive information. They may also install a program called a trojan horse that is designed to act as a back door into the system while appearing to perform a benign function.

For cybersoldiers, the goal of cyber espionage would be to learn about a potential enemy's planned operations before they can be set into motion. Cybersoldiers engaged in cyber espionage would need serious hacking skills. They also would have to be briefed on what type of information to look for and how to relay such information back to their superiors.

WEB VANDALISM AND PROPAGANDA

One of the most visible ways for cyberterrorists to make their mark is by vandalizing high-profile Web sites. Hackers interested in making brazen political statements sometimes crack the Web site of a major corporation or government entity and change it to reflect their own views and make their target appear foolish. On the surface, such actions may seem to do little to hurt the target except inconvenience the programmers who have to fix the site and update security protocols. However, acts of Web vandalism can be a powerful motivator. If the vandal chooses the right target, the vandalized Web site could be seen by millions of people before it is taken down and repaired. Acts of Web vandalism can also show a group's

Videos of hostages often appear on terrorist Web sites aimed at recruiting new followers. Such videos serve a double purpose by also inspiring copycat terrorist acts.

followers that it is not afraid to commit brazen acts, suggesting that more daring and direct action may follow.

Well-publicized acts of Web vandalism can prove to be excellent propaganda tools for a terrorist group and shore up the commitment of its followers while bringing in new recruits. In fact, propaganda campaigns that use the Internet can awaken interest in a terrorist group in otherwise indifferent individuals.

Cyberterrorists also use their own Web pages, message boards, social networking sites, and other Internet entities to spread their message. Conventional terrorist groups use these sites to boast about their activities and slam their enemies. They may post videos of hostages or footage of attacks and often use the Internet to claim responsibility for acts of terrorism.

Just as cyberterrorists hack into networks to learn about potential targets, cybersoldiers can learn about terrorists and their plots by closely monitoring message boards and Web sites. They often comb through the online chatter in search of credible threats or information that can lead to action against terrorists and their groups.

Cybersoldiers can also hack into terrorist Web sites to discover who established them, though the terrorists make this difficult by concealing their identities beneath multiple layers of misdirection. However, a successful hacking mission can sometimes lead back to terrorist computer networks. The cybersoldiers can then establish a trojan horse in the network that allows them to learn more about the terrorists, or they can bring the network down by introducing a virus or other malicious program.

HARDWARE ATTACKS

While cyberterrorists do much of their damage through the Internet, they sometimes use corrupted computer hardware to compromise networks. Hardware includes anything that is part of the physical computer, such as computer chips and the hard drive. It would be technically difficult and risky for a terrorist to take apart a computer belonging to the government and exchange functional hardware components for some that have been corrupted with a virus, trojan horse, or data-mining program.

However, it is easy to distribute portable storage hardware, such as CDs and flash drives, or use such devices to spread malicious software programs. Corrupted flash drives or CDs containing viruses or malware can easily be switched or mixed in with legitimate storage hardware that looks similar. In other cases, corrupted storage devices may simply be left for antiterrorist forces or curious individuals to find. Sometimes, a user may not even realize that he or she has exposed the network or computer to corrupted hardware devices.

The programs contained on these devices could pose numerous threats to a network. They could be designed to aggressively attack the network with viruses and shut it down. Trojan horse programs left on these devices could give cyberterrorists a back door to the network. Data mining programs could allow cyberterrorists to quietly gather information from the network without interfering with other programs.

Cyberterrorists may also gain direct access to computers by misrepresenting themselves as outside contractors or technical support staff. Under the cover of making repairs or updating hardware, they may be left undisturbed long enough to tamper with hardware. While such an operation may appear brazen, the cyberterrorist may assume that few would question the presence of contractors or technical support personnel.

Hardware attacks would be much more difficult for cybersoldiers to carry out. The cybersoldiers would need direct access to computers used by terrorists or areas that they frequent. The effort necessary to get close enough to distribute corrupted hardware could be greater than the benefit, though there is some potential for distributing corrupted storage devices.

THE BLACK HAT CONFERENCE

The Black Hat Conference is a major event attended by people interested in various aspects of computer security, including representatives from corporations and federal agencies, as well as hackers. Black Hat was founded in 1997 by a hacker named Jeff Moss as a way for experts in these somewhat divergent fields to share their knowledge. Since then, the conference has grown to include thousands of participants annually.

The conference consists of briefings and training. Briefings cover topics such as reverse engineering and identity and privacy, and feature keynote speeches from leading experts in information security. The hands-on training sessions are provided by information security experts and security corporations. Attendees can even receive professional certification from some of the training sessions offered. Hackers attending the conference disclose security weaknesses they have discovered. In recent years, the conference has become a destination for government agencies looking to recruit bright hackers for cybersecurity and cyber warfare programs.

DENIAL-OF-SERVICE ATTACKS

One of the most effective methods used by cyberterrorists is the denial-of-service attack. A denial-of-service attack consists of a concerted effort by individuals to prevent an Internet site or service from functioning properly and therefore rendering it unusable to regular users for a temporary or indefinite period of time. Cyberterrorists often target services or sites hosted on high-profile servers, such as banks or credit card payment gateways.

One method of carrying out a denial-of-service attack is to bombard the site or service with external communication requests, cutting it off from legitimate Web traffic or slowing it to such an extent that it essentially becomes unavailable. The attacks either force the targeted computer to reset, consume its resources so that it cannot provide its intended service, or obstruct communications between the site and its users.

These attacks may be coordinated between multiple cyberterrorists or carried out by a single individual using a program designed to overwhelm the site or consume its resources. Attacks carried out by multiple cyberterrorists are called distributed denial-of-service attacks. These attacks consist of multiple systems flooding the bandwidth of a targeted system, such as a Web server. In some cases, cyberterrorists infect multiple computers with programs called malware, which hijack infected computers and use them to carry out attacks without the user's knowledge. Such attacks are more difficult to shut down than regular denial-of-service attacks because of the sheer number of attacking systems and the fact that most participants have no idea they are unwittingly taking part in a cyberterror attack.

Several major distributed denial-of-service attacks have made headlines in recent years. The cyber attack against Estonia used this tactic, and similar attacks were launched against sites in the United States and South Korea the same year. Criminal organizations in Russia were suspected of orchestrating denial-of-service attacks against government Web sites maintained by the Republic of Georgia in the weeks leading up to the 2008 South Ossetia War.

Denial-of-service incidents can take place by accident when a particularly high number of users visit a site all at once. In one famous example, a spike in Web users searching for information at the time of pop star Michael Jackson's death in June 2009 caused the Web news aggregating site Google News to briefly shut down because administrators suspected a denial-of-service attack was taking place.

Distributed denial-of-service attacks have little practical application for cybersoldiers. Carrying out such an attack against sites and services used by terrorists would be impractical. Terrorists often relocate their Web sites, and attacks against message boards used by terrorists would also lock out legitimate users. Denial-of-service attacks are considered violations by Internet-regulating authorities such as the Internet Architecture Board, and they violate acceptable use policies of most Internet service providers. Several nations consider these attacks violations of their laws. Rather than carrying out their own denial-of-service attacks, cybersoldiers must use other tactics, such as cyber espionage, to learn of such attacks before they can take place and warn any potential targets. However, the U.S. government has not committed to ruling out such attacks against cyberterrorists in the future.

CHAPTER 3
Military Careers

As of 2010, the most developed career path for potential cyber-soldiers is through the military. While the U.S. government and military establishment have been criticized as being slow to act against cyberterrorism, the armed forces remain among the few places where potential cybersoldiers can receive formal training in the field. As the military continues to develop its dependence on computer technology, it will likely place a larger emphasis on training cybersoldiers to help it gain a greater technological edge over the nation's enemies.

The military itself has been vulnerable to attacks by cyberterrorists. Multiple attempts have been made in recent years to attack networks belonging to the Department of Defense. In December 2009, the military confirmed that Iraqi insurgents had used an inexpensive software program to exploit unprotected communication links and successfully hack into video feeds captured by unmanned aerial surveillance vehicles flying over Iraq. As the military works to end such security lapses, its various branches have each begun to establish their own cybersoldier forces as a way to provide a deterrent to would-be attackers and strike cyberterrorists before they can attack.

The Pentagon is working to develop techniques to damage an enemy's computer networks so badly that they will be unable to function. The military wants this ability to keep enemies from accessing and using critical information and services and

In a 2008 speech, General David Cartwright of the Department of Defense's Joint Chiefs of Staff discusses the importance of experimenting with cyber warfare on the battlefield.

to alter their data to trick enemies with false information. In war zones in Iraq and Afghanistan, military commanders are already working to disrupt the ability of enemy commanders to direct their forces by shutting off electricity and communication lines and manipulating data. Most of the tactics that are in use or that are being developed remain classified.

ARMY

The army is the oldest branch of the military, dating back to the Revolutionary War (1775–1783). Its soldiers take part in military actions, peacekeeping missions, and humanitarian efforts around the world. Despite its willingness and ability to adapt to unique situations on the field and use the latest high-tech equipment, the army's high command has the reputation of being slow to respond to threats in cyberspace. However, that has begun to change as more high-profile cyber attacks occur.

In 2009, the army completed a draft of a manual for engaging in cyber warfare. The document attempts to account for scenarios ranging from stopping hackers from taking over networks to monitoring electronic communications between enemies. It includes instructions for dealing with situations ranging from concerted attacks by well-trained cyberterrorists to curious high school students attempting to hack into government sites. It also contains principles for battlefield commanders using computers and information technology to identify enemies, communicate with soldiers, and inform allies of the military's actions.

Most details regarding how the army will put its cyber-soldiers to work are classified or undeveloped, although the draft does provide a basic outline. Each army unit regardless of size will have networking computer systems, trained personnel capable of using them for communications, and cyber warfare applications. Their goal would be to keep the enemy from operating in cyberspace by denying access to a network, influencing how and what their devices transmit, and disabling computers by destroying hardware or erasing data.

AIR FORCE

The air force was established in 1947, when it split off from the army. The new branch of the military was seen as the future of warfare, enabling the nation to strike against enemies from afar without mobilizing large ground forces. The air force has long been quick to adopt new technology to improve its jets and weapons, transportation, and communications systems, and it relies heavily on computer technology. Because of this reliance, the air force was the first branch of the military to realize the importance of establishing a cyber warfare program.

In 2006, the air force announced that it was creating a new Cyberspace Command unit, designated the 8th Air Force. The unit was set up to defend networks, reinforce communications through cyberspace, carry out cyber warfare missions against enemies, and use cyberspace to gather intelligence. Airmen would be trained as cybersoldiers through the air force's own education system.

Members of the U.S. Air Force's electronic warfare teams monitor a simulated test at Eglin Air Force Base in Florida. The air force has developed the military's most extensive cyber warfare program.

When it was first envisioned, the Cyberspace Command unit was expected to consist of several hundred staff overseeing a possible twenty thousand air force personnel. These would include software experts, lawyers, electronic warfare and satellite experts, and behavioral scientists. However, the unit was ordered to shut down in 2008, just weeks before it was scheduled to become fully operational, while the air force's high command rethought its scope and mission. In the interim, the Cyber Command was established, ending the air force's quest to become the nation's leader in cyber warfare operations.

In 2009, the 24th Air Force unit was formed to provide combat-ready forces trained and equipped to carry out cyber warfare operations in coordination with air and space operations. The unit's mission includes instantaneously setting up new networks in war zones and protecting the air force's existing networks. The unit will also oversee network training for incoming recruits and officer candidates. This training will include proper use of flash drives and participation in cyber war simulations.

One of the training centers for air force cybersoldiers is the Air Force Institute of Technology, located at Wright-Patterson Air Force Base in Ohio. The institute houses the air force's Center for Cyberspace Research, which was founded in 2002 to conduct defense-focused research at the graduate and doctorate levels.

NAVY

The navy has come a long way from the days of wooden ships and sails. Today's navy uses networks to find targets, launch

A naval information systems technician uses an intrusion detection system to monitor unclassified network activity aboard the aircraft carrier USS Ronald Reagan. Such systems protect networks from attack.

weapons, communicate, and navigate. In January 2010, the navy joined the army and air force in establishing its own cyber warfare organization under the Cyber Command. The U.S. Fleet/U.S. 10th Fleet's mission will be similar to the missions of the cyber warfare units of the army and air force. It will work to detect and defend against potential intrusions on Department of Defense networks and conduct its own operations.

The U.S. Navy Cyber Force will include cryptology, signals intelligence, electronic warfare, information operations, intelligence, networks, and space disciplines. Its mission will include prioritizing and organizing manpower, training, modernization and maintenance requirements, capabilities of networks, oversight of cryptologic and space-related systems, and intelligence and information operations activities. The force will carry out network and space operations for all forces afloat and on shore.

The U.S. Naval Academy in Annapolis, Maryland, operates its Center for Cybersecurity Studies to enhance the education of naval midshipmen in all areas relating to cyber security. The Naval Academy is considering plans to make cybersecurity a core aspect of the education of its potential officers by requiring that its midshipmen take at least one course in cybersecurity.

JOINING THE MILITARY

Life in the military can be physically, mentally, and emotionally demanding. Every branch has its own particular requirements. For potential cybersoldiers seeking to join the military, the requirements may be more specific than for regular recruits.

All new military recruits must meet certain physical standards. They must undergo complete physical examinations and psychological testing. They must also pass background checks. New recruits must be at least seventeen years old and hold a high school diploma, though the standard is occasionally waived for exceptional recruits with a General Educational Development (GED) diploma. If they have dependents, such as a spouse or children, they must prove that they can provide for their care. Recruits have to be U.S. citizens or have resident alien status. While noncitizens can

Cyber war training courses at the Space and Naval Warfare Systems Center are designed to teach personnel to defend networks with sweeps and scans of the system and respond to viruses.

enlist, they are not permitted to reenlist unless they first become naturalized citizens. Citizens of some nations considered hostile to the United States may need a special waiver before they can enlist.

Before joining, potential recruits must take a standardized test called the Armed Services Vocational Aptitude Battery, or ASVAB. The test covers general science, arithmetic reasoning, vocabulary, reading comprehension, mathematics, electronics, auto and shop knowledge, and mechanical comprehension. Test scores help determine which military jobs would be the best fit for a potential recruit.

Physical standards differ for each military branch and can be provided by local recruiting offices. For the most part, people interested in joining the military must be in good physical condition, with no serious chronic health problems such as diabetes or heart conditions. The physical examination includes height and weight measurements, vision and hearing exams, blood and urine tests, testing for alcohol and drugs, and examination of the muscles and joints.

After taking the ASVAB and passing the physical examination, the recruit meets with a service enlistment counselor in order to find the right job specialty. Factors that help determine a recruit's military position include the needs of the service, job availability, ASVAB scores, physical requirements of the job, and the recruit's preference. Since the army, navy, and air force are ramping up their cyber warfare operations, potential cyber-soldiers who do well on the ASVAB and pass all of the other requirements are likely to land cyber warfare jobs in the service.

Once a recruit has been accepted, he or she must complete basic training, which consists of a combination of physical training, classes, and field exercises. The process is intended to make recruits stronger and capable of carrying out a variety of maneuvers in the field and teach them to work together. Basic training lasts for nine weeks in the army, eight-and-a-half weeks in the air force, and eight weeks in the navy.

Once basic training is complete, service members receive training in their assigned military career field. The recruits learn about their careers through classes, field instruction, and hands-on training. Some recruits considered to be officer candidates will go on to similar training with a greater leadership component. Typically, officer candidates are recruits with college degrees or specialized training.

U.S. CYBER COMMAND

In June 2009, Secretary of Defense Robert Gates created the U.S. Cyber Command to coordinate computer network defenses between the branches of the military and direct cyber attacks. In May 2010, the National Security Agency director, General Keith Alexander, was confirmed as its commander.

During his confirmation hearings before the U.S. Senate, Alexander warned that policies and legal controls over digital combat are outdated and lag behind advances in military technology. Responding to questions from senators, Alexander described his vision for cyber warfare, including traditional military targets such as air defense networks and weapons systems that require computers to operate. He also said that a potential target list could include civilian institutions and infrastructure such as banks and power grids, but that the command would attempt to limit the impact on civilians.

TRAINING IN THE ARMY

Army recruits go to Advanced Individual Training School, where they are trained in one of seventeen career fields ranging from artillery to finance. The army has been secretive regarding the sort of training that recruits receive for cyber warfare. Recruits interested in cyber warfare will likely enter the army's computers and technology career track. The army has twenty-four distinct careers for individuals interested in computers and technology, ranging from systems operations and diagnostics to multimedia illustration.

Two army career fields are currently committed to cyberspace operations: the Signal Corps and the Military Intelligence

Corps. The Signal Corps is responsible for providing and managing communications and information systems support for the command and control of combined armed forces, including computer networks. The Military Intelligence Corps is responsible for providing timely, relevant, and accurate intelligence and electronic warfare support. Intelligence officers lead, manage, and direct intelligence planning and operations.

INTELLIGENCE ANALYSTS

Army intelligence analysts are responsible for providing army personnel with information regarding enemy forces and potential battle sites. They use information gathered from all intelligence disciplines to determine changes in enemy capabilities, vulnerabilities, and probable courses of action. They receive and process incoming reports and messages, help determine the importance and reliability of incoming information, establish and maintain intelligence records and files, and integrate incoming information with current information, and prepare and maintain graphics.

Training consists of thirteen weeks beyond basic training and will cover maps and charts, preparing intelligence reports, military symbiology, critical thinking, and an introduction to the army's Distributed Common Ground System. Recruits interested in becoming intelligence analysts should have an interest in reading maps and charts and in gathering information and studying its meaning. Information-gathering techniques include infiltration of computer and communication networks to intercept messages. They also should be able to organize information and think and communicate clearly. Advance level intelligence analysts are experienced in the field and responsible for training others. They supervise intelligence surveillance, assess enemy vulnerabilities and probable courses of action, assist in preparing reports on captured enemy material, and plan intelligence-gathering actions.

COUNTERINTELLIGENCE AGENTS

The position of counterintelligence agent is available to more experienced soldiers. Counterintelligence agents work to protect national defense information, including electronic information, from enemies, foreign intelligence agents, and terrorists. Intelligence specialists such as counterintelligence agents provide army personnel with information about enemy intelligence capability and intent and counter those capabilities. Counterintelligence agents are responsible for supervising and conducting counterintelligence surveys and investigations to detect, identify, assess, counter, exploit, and neutralize these threats.

Duties of counterintelligence agents may include investigations of national security crimes such as espionage, treason, and subversion, processing counterintelligence evidence, preparing and distributing counterintelligence reports to relevant parties, providing counterintelligence support to antiterrorism operations, conducting liaison operations, and maintaining counterintelligence files and databases. Helpful skills include an interest in reading maps and charts and gathering intelligence and interpreting its meaning, an ability to think and write clearly and organize information, and an outgoing personality.

Job training for counterintelligence agents requires nineteen weeks of attendance at the Counterintelligence Special

Agent Course and on-the-job instruction, including practice in counterintelligence investigations, operations, and analysis. Part of this time is spent in the classroom and part in the field. Skills covered in the training include evidence collection; interviewing techniques; preparing maps, charts, and intelligence reports; and using computer systems.

TRAINING IN THE AIR FORCE

After finishing with basic training, air force recruits begin technical training to learn the skills they will need to perform their jobs. Technical training takes place at five different air force bases: Goodfellow, Lackland, and Sheppard air force bases in Texas; Keesler Air Force Base in Mississippi; and Vandenberg Air Force Base in California. Though its anticipated cybercommand has been greatly reduced, the air force still has the military's most advanced cyber warfare service.

Keesler Air Force Base is the official headquarters for the air force's cyber warfare training program. In August 2009, its cyber warfare program welcomed its first ninety-five recruits. The air force expects to train about 4,500 airmen in cyber warfare annually. Training at Keesler includes a six-month initial skills course for about four hundred officers and enlisted personnel who show particular promise in cyber warfare. About half of the training is conducted in a top secret facility. The final segment of the training uses mission simulators to replicate a cyber attack to test the responses of the students. Those who do well will receive further cyber warfare training.

When they complete the six- to fifteen-month training program, the new cybersoldiers will likely join the 24th Air

Force. The unit is made up of three cyber wings: the 688th Information Operations Wing, the 67th Network Warfare Wing, and the 689th Combat Communications Wing.

The mission of the 67th Network Warfare Wing, located in Texas, is to organize, train, and equip cyberspace forces to conduct network defense, attack, and exploitation. It also executes full-spectrum air force network operations, training, tactics, and management tasks. The wing has more than eight thousand personnel, and its members and equipment are located all over the world to provide information to the nation's leaders.

The 688th Information Operations Wing is a re-designation of the air force's Information Operations Center and consists of about one thousand personnel. The wing is responsible for creating information operations advantages for combatant forces by exploring, developing, applying, and transitioning counter information technology, strategy, tactics, and data to control the cyber warfare arena.

The 689th Combat Communications Wing consists of about seven thousand personnel and is responsible for training, deploying, and delivering the air force's warfighter expeditionary communications, information systems, engineering and installation, air traffic control, and weather services. The wing is largely responsible for supporting the other two wings.

TRAINING IN THE NAVY

When navy recruits complete basic training, they attend "A" School, where they learn the specific duties that go with their career paths. "A" Schools are located in coastal regions throughout the country. "A" School is divided into three phases and typically lasts for twelve weeks, but it can last longer if a recruit is not ready to move on to the next phase. Some navy personnel go on to even more training after finishing "A" School.

The navy's 10th Fleet Cyber Command includes information warfare and intelligence officers, enlisted intelligence, information technology personnel, and cryptologic technicians. For naval officers joining the navy's cyber force in the 10th Fleet, training takes place at the Navy Information Operations Command Center in Maryland.

Enlisted intelligence work includes a great deal of training in the use and maintenance of sophisticated equipment. Specialized navy personnel in this field track targets, analyze intelligence, maintain Combat Information Center displays of strategic and tactical information, serve as air traffic controllers, operate and maintain global satellite systems, work with classified material, provide support to forces in the field, and operate radio and computer equipment.

Information technology personnel are largely responsible for maintaining and securing networks and technology. The work of cryptologic technicians focuses on cryptology signals information tasks. Specialists in this field work at administrative and clerical duties controlling access to classified information, perform interpretations of communications, maintain equipment, perform network functions in support of defending or exploiting network systems, and operate communications equipment. Cryptologic technicians are responsible for electronic defense and electronic attacks, as well as electronic warfare support.

CHAPTER 4

Government and Law Enforcement Careers

While the military's cyber warfare programs continue to grow, cyber warfare programs in the government and law enforcement also show promise. The government's Department of Homeland Security and Department of Defense have a particular interest in combating cyberterrorism. The Central Intelligence Agency (CIA) and law enforcement agencies such as the Federal Bureau of Investigation (FBI) that are working to disrupt large-scale criminal operations will likely have to rely on advanced cyber warfare techniques as criminal networks become more sophisticated in their own cyber operations.

Computer operating systems are vulnerable to hackers, foreign agents, business firms that install usage trackers, data thieves, and terrorists. Basic security steps include setting up firewalls, using passwords and changing them often, using encryption, and avoiding suspicious Internet links. Internet service providers are also vulnerable to attack and maintain their own security measures. Government network security is much more sophisticated than security for most private and commercial networks, but its facilities remain vulnerable.

WHEN ATTACKS OCCUR

Even the most secure networks can fall to cyberterrorists if the right weaknesses are found and exploited. The U.S.

Internet security has been a global problem since the 1990s. Today, skilled hackers can make thousands of dollars a day working from places such as this Internet café located in Africa's Ivory Coast.

government has spent billions on security for its many networks. However, attacks on the security of these networks occur frequently.

As early as February 1998, when the U.S. military was preparing for a four-day bombing campaign against targets in Iraq, the Department of Defense discovered that intruders had broken into numerous, seemingly secure department computers by obtaining root access that would allow them to steal or alter information and damage networks.

The attacks continued for about a month. Officials suspected that the Iraqi government was behind the intrusions and worried that the intruders had stolen the bombing plans. The intrusions were traced to an Internet service provider (ISP) in the Persian Gulf, and countermeasures were considered, including bombing the perceived source of the intrusions.

Eventually, the intrusions were traced to two California teenagers and an Israeli teenager hacking into the department's network using the Persian Gulf ISP. The incident demonstrated some of the shortcomings of network security at the time and showed that intrusions did not necessarily have to come from well-organized networks with malicious intent. However, networks across the country remain vulnerable to attack. These targets have included nuclear power plants, financial institutions, and intelligence agencies. The Department of Defense remains a favorite target.

Attackers can range from curious hackers attempting to penetrate protected systems to prove that they can or to commit malicious acts to those criminals who might steal sensitive personal information or money or commit acts of commercial or government espionage. To the government, the cyber attack threat that poses the most substantial risk comes from terrorists.

KNOWN ATTACKS

The 1998 Department of Defense intrusions were among the first cyber attacks against the government to receive major publicity, though the attacks themselves were not committed by cyberterrorists. Since then, the number and intensity of attacks have grown significantly. In May 2009, networks belonging to the FBI and the U.S. Marshals Service were hit by an aggressive computer virus that forced the agencies to shut down their external networks while they investigated. Both law enforcement agencies are frequent targets of hackers from criminal organizations, terrorist networks, and foreign intelligence agencies working to steal classified information or disrupt their work.

A 2010 FBI report revealed that since 2003, the Chinese government has developed a force of 180,000 cyber spies, including 30,000 in the Chinese military and 150,000 in the private sector. This massive force has launched ninety thousand attacks a year against Defense Department computers alone and could disrupt banking and commerce, destroy vital infrastructure, and compromise sensitive military and defense databases. In 2007 and 2009, Chinese hackers were able to breach Pentagon network security systems and access information that included designs for the military's Joint Strike Fighter project.

According to the FBI, the attacks have mostly been aimed at gathering information about the U.S. military and intercepting data collected by security agencies such as the NSA.

The U.S. Air Force's Joint Strike Fighter program resulted in the development of the F-35 Lightning II stealth fighter. Plans for the advanced aircraft were accessed by hackers in 2007 and 2009.

Many of the detected cyber attacks against the military consist of hackers embedding programs into government networks that search for information and then e-mailing it back to China. The hackers are skilled at implanting malicious computer code, and in 2009, a number of U.S. companies in industries such as banking, aerospace, energy, and telecommunications reported significant and costly problems with malware that originated in China.

U.S. agencies have launched their own successful cyber attacks. In 2007, shortly before the military began a major troop buildup against insurgents in Iraq, the NSA launched a sophisticated attack aimed at disrupting insurgent communications.

The attack targeted cell phones and computers used by insurgents to plan roadside bombs. The operation allowed U.S. forces to take control of the communication systems used by the insurgents and use the devices to spread confusion and false information, leading the insurgents into the line of fire.

Along with military institutions, government agencies are on the front lines of potential cyber warfare. These include any number of U.S. intelligence agencies, many of which are linked through the government's Department of Homeland Security. The U.S. intelligence community promises to be a rich area for potential cybersoldiers who want to find work in the field without joining the military. Agencies with active

National Security Agency (NSA) employees work in the agency's Threat Response Center. The NSA responded to a 2009 cyber attack that knocked out the Web sites of several government agencies.

cyber departments include the FBI, the CIA, the NSA, and the Department of Homeland Security. Cybersoldiers who join these agencies can expect to be in the forefront of the government's strategies for contending with cyberattacks.

JOBS IN THE FBI

The FBI is the law enforcement and domestic intelligence agency responsible for protecting the nation against terrorist and foreign intelligence threats; upholding and enforcing federal laws; and assisting other local, state, and federal law enforcement agencies. The FBI's priorities include protecting the nation from terrorist attacks, espionage, and high-tech and cyber crimes, along with protecting civil rights. The FBI combats public corruption, transnational and national crime syndicates, and white-collar crime and significant violent crime. It also works to upgrade technology to assist its agents in carrying out their missions. The agency's headquarters are located in Washington, D.C., and there are fifty-six FBI field offices in cities across the United States and Puerto Rico.

The FBI's focus on using information technology to meet its priorities led it to create its own cyber division in 2002. The division addresses crimes with a cyber connection or core. These violations often have international facets and implications for the nation's economy. The division also assists in counterterrorism investigations, counterintelligence, and other operations in which there is a need for aggressive technological investigation assistance.

The division coordinates, supervises, and facilitates the FBI's investigation of those federal violations in which the Internet, computer systems, or networks are attacked. The targets of the division's work can include terrorist organizations, foreign government–sponsored intelligence operations, or criminals who need such systems to commit their crimes. The division is also responsible for making sure that the FBI's own information technology and tactics remain up-to-date and capable of allowing alliances with private companies in order to receive additional training and improve cyber response capabilities.

DIVISION REQUIREMENTS

The FBI has a variety of jobs available in numerous fields, so there is no single type of degree or prior work experience that may be better than others for getting work in the bureau. However, people with specific career goals within the agency will need the relevant education or experience to follow those paths. Within the Cyber Division, opportunities are available for people interested in investigating cyber crimes and computer intrusions, as well as applicants with an interest in special technologies and applications and in information sharing and analysis. The FBI hires information technology specialists in applications software, database management, network engineering, operating systems, policy and planning, program and project management, software engineering, systems administration, and systems analysis.

Special agents in the division have undergraduate, graduate, and doctoral degrees in computer science, information technology, and related engineering fields. The division has expanded its intelligence component and is seeking candidates with intelligence-related education, training, and backgrounds consistent with the FBI's standards.

OPERATION BOT ROAST

Operation Bot Roast was a major project undertaken by the FBI in 2007, with the goal of tracking down and prosecuting hackers who install malicious software called bots on the computers of unsuspecting users. When the bots are activated, they allow the hackers to control the computers. Hackers who have compromised enough computers can build networks called botnets consisting of thousands of machines. These computers can then be used to carry out denial-of-service attacks, send spam messages, and commit other cyber crimes without the knowledge of their owners.

Through Operation Bot Roast, the FBI was able to identify more than one million computers that had been compromised. The agency also identified a number of cyber criminals called bot herders and brought charges against them.

The division requires personnel with education, training, and practical work experience in computer science and information technology. Applicants with private sector, government, and military experience in those fields are desired. Critical skill areas include engineering, hardware and software design, and operating systems analysis.

The division also provides cutting-edge training through government programs and partnerships with private companies. Training opportunities for division employees range from in-house training in cyber basics to advanced technical training. Employees are regularly required to update their knowledge due to the rapid pace of innovations in software and hardware technology.

BUREAU REQUIREMENTS AND TRAINING

Applying to join the FBI can be a long process. Because all FBI positions call for at least a top secret security clearance, the bureau does extensive background testing and automatically disqualifies candidates who have been convicted of a felony, fail a drug test, have some drug use in their backgrounds, and have defaulted on their federal student loans, as well as men who have failed to register with the Selective Service. Applicants must also prove that they are U.S. citizens. Applicants who are citizens but hold dual citizenship in another country are eligible, but they must submit to further screening by the bureau's security division. Applicants must also meet certain physical and medical criteria.

The bureau hires new agents all year long, but because it requires a background check and high-level security clearance for all agents, it is best for an applicant to apply for a position at least six to nine months before he or she wants to start working. The background investigation includes a polygraph test, drug test, interviews with current and former friends and acquaintances, and credit and records checks. The time that it takes to conduct the investigation differs between candidates and can depend on several factors, such as how many different places the applicant has lived and how many jobs the applicant has held.

All agents receive intensive on-the-job training when they begin work at the bureau. Applicants who are interested in becoming special agents, intelligence analysts, language analysts, and investigative/surveillance specialists must undergo extensive training at the FBI Academy in Quantico, Virginia.

Qualified special agent applicants are invited to take a multiple-choice test that gauges cognitive skills and situational judgment. Some applicants are nominated for the second phase of testing, which includes an interview with a panel of agents and a written essay. Those who pass phase two testing, as well as various other procedures such as a polygraph test, drug testing, background check, and a security interview, officially become new agent trainees. The next step is a sixteen-week training period at the FBI Academy.

Once they're on the job, recruits generally spend a two-year probation period under the supervision of a field training officer. They are often assigned to six to twelve months in the application squad, where they perform background checks on job applicants for federal positions. This stint, a good starting point for new agents, gives them a chance to improve their investigative skills and familiarize themselves with FBI procedures. Special agents should be willing to relocate whenever they are assigned or transferred to a different office.

Promotions are decided by career boards made up of senior FBI personnel. Most agents spend their entire careers as FBI special agents, often developing specialized skills and taking on further responsibilities through their years of experience. Some agents apply for a promotion to the position of supervisory special agent, the head of a squad within a field office. The top position at an FBI field office is the special agent in charge (SAC). The SAC oversees all FBI activities carried out in the field office's area of operations, whether it's a city, state, or group of states.

CAREERS WITH THE CIA

The CIA's main mission is to collect intelligence on foreign governments, individuals, and corporations, and advise public policy makers. The agency also performs covert operations and paramilitary actions, and it works to influence foreign governments.

The agency's cyber capabilities are centralized in a unit called the Information Operations System Analysis Group. This unit evaluates foreign threats to the nation's computer systems, particularly those that support critical infrastructure. The unit provides analysis of these threats to the president, his senior advisers, high-level officials on cyber issues in the Departments of State, Treasury, and Defense, and to senior private-sector officials responsible for operating critical infrastructures. Analysts within the unit consider potential threats from other countries and terrorists and analyze their intentions, strategies, and capabilities.

Cybersoldiers with the CIA may be employed as intelligence collection analysts. In this position, they apply their expertise on intelligence collection systems capabilities, processes, and policies to drive the flow of intelligence information and provide the data needed to understand and analyze issues to colleagues. Others may work as counterintelligence threat analysts who collect, study, and interpret a range of reports to identify and prevent foreign intelligence operations that threaten the government or intelligence community. Counterterrorism analysts help warn of terrorist threats by assessing the leadership, motivations, plans, and intentions of foreign terrorist groups and their state and nonstate sponsors.

Cybersoldiers may find work at the agency as science and technology analysts. Analysts with a background in computers and information technology may use their knowledge to identify and analyze possible weapons proliferation and proliferators, conventional weapons systems, information warfare, computer systems, and energy security. Targeting analysts can use network analysis techniques and specialized analytical tools to identify and detail key figures and organizations that may pose a threat to U.S. interests.

Computer forensics is one area in which the CIA is looking to expand within its science and technology division. CIA computer forensics engineers examine electronic media to assess and prioritize their intelligence value. They examine computer-based electronic media such as CDs and hard drives for configuration files, system files, and registry information from operating systems, user-created documents, network routing, and content information.

Computer forensics engineers use assessment tools and operating systems to examine and process this data. They also research and analyze new computer and data security tools and applications to determine how they are used. They develop new tools and methods for processing and analyzing data and for keeping up-to-date on digital forensics techniques. Computer forensics engineers develop strategic assessments about trends, usage, and threats based on patterns, which are used to educate the intelligence community on threats and cyber profiles.

Candidates for computer forensics jobs with the CIA need five years of experience in computer security, computer forensics, computer investigations, or a related technical field. Candidates should have a working knowledge of multiple operating systems, file systems, media types, and programming languages. Applicants need a working knowledge of the Internet and related technologies, such as firewalls, intrusion detection systems, computer security tools, and encryption systems. They also should have a working knowledge of counterintelligence techniques and the ability to read, translate, and analyze data in a foreign language.

APPLYING TO THE CIA

All CIA applicants must complete a thorough medical and psychological evaluation, submit to a polygraph test, and pass a drug test. To be considered, applicants must be U.S. citizens and submit to a background examination. The agency asks applicants to use discretion and good judgment regarding the application process, since applicants can't control whether or not their friends and relatives tell others.

The background check examines an applicant's loyalty to the United States, strength of character, trustworthiness, honesty, reliability, discretion, and soundness of judgment. In addition, it examines his or her freedom from conflicting allegiances, potential for coercion, and willingness and ability to abide by regulations governing the use, handling, and protection of sensitive information. The agency uses polygraphs to test the truth of any information relating to these criteria. Once applicants are hired, they have to submit to regular reinvestigations, including occasional polygraph tests. Travel is often required.

The agency offers multiple internships and job opportunities to college undergraduates. High school seniors planning to enroll in a four- or five-year college program and college sophomores already enrolled in such a program can apply for the CIA's Undergraduate Scholarship Program. Students who are accepted into the program spend each summer break working for the agency in a field related to their major. An information technology major, for example, would likely work on increasingly complex projects using advanced computer systems. Applicants must pass the same criteria as regular employees, demonstrate financial need, and maintain a 3.0 grade point average during the school year.

JOBS WITH THE NATIONAL SECURITY AGENCY

The NSA is responsible for collecting and analyzing foreign communications and intercepting and analyzing communication signals. The agency also protects the nation's communications and information systems from similar organizations associated with other governments. Since 2008, the NSA has been the lead agency for protecting federal computer networks from cyberterrorists. The agency's mission statement includes the goal of enabling network warfare operations to give the United States and its allies an advantage.

The agency has a great demand for cybersoldiers in its computer network operations career path. Computer science professionals are hired for computer network attacks, network defense, and network exploitation. Computer network attacks involve disrupting, denying, degrading, or destroying information within computers and computer networks, or the destruction of the computers or networks themselves. Network defense requires analyzing, protecting against, and responding to network attacks, intrusions, disruptions, and other actions that could compromise or cripple defense information systems and networks. Network exploitation includes actions and intelligence collection via computers that exploit data gathered from target or enemy information systems or networks.

Individuals interested in working for the NSA must submit their applications online, where they will enter the agency's database. The agency checks applications against any job

An FBI recruit takes part in target practice. Recruits who want to become special agents are required to go through a grueling training course at the FBI Academy.

openings and contacts qualified applicants. If contacted, applicants must undergo a medical exam, polygraph test, drug test, and an extensive background check. To be eligible, applicants must prove U.S. citizenship.

HOMELAND SECURITY

The Department of Homeland Security is a sprawling government department made up of many different federal agencies responsible for protecting the nation against terrorist attacks and natural disasters. The department's cyber capabilities are contained within its National Cyber Security Division. The division's goal is to protect the country's cyber infrastructure by building and maintaining effective national cyberspace response and cyberspace risk management systems. The response system mobilizes personnel and programs in the event of a cyber incident, while the risk management system is designed to help the agency analyze risks and determine appropriate responses.

Cyber jobs with the department include work with the Computer Emergency Readiness Team (CERT). CERT is a partnership between the department and the private sector that was created in 2003 to coordinate the response to security threats through the Internet. The National Cyber Response Coordination Group is the main federal agency mechanism for coordinating a response to a cyber incident. In the event of a nationally significant cyber incident, the group organizes the actions of thirteen federal agencies, including CERT, law enforcement, and intelligence agencies. Employment with the department requires background checks and physical exams, as well as any specific requirements for individual agencies.

CHAPTER 5

Preparing for a Cybersoldier Career

Cyber warfare is a new and unconventional career field. Outside of the military and government work, it has very few legal applications in the United States. Specialized training in the field is limited largely to the federal government and the military. Most cybersoldiers today have their education background in conventional computer science, information technology, or computer engineering, often with a focus on security.

COMPUTER SCIENCE PROGRAMS

Computer science is the study of the mathematical theories and practices used to create, transmit, transform, and describe information within computer systems. The field has many subfields that aim to solve specific computational problems, yield results in a particular way, or improve the way in which people interact with computers. Computer science studies the properties of programs that are used to implement software such as Web browsers and games.

Computer science programs are widespread and can be found at four-year colleges, two-year technical and vocational schools, and at the graduate level at many universities. Some university programs emphasize the theoretical study of computing. This education path includes theories of computation, analysis of mathematical algorithms, systems analysis,

High school computer classes can teach students interested in becoming cybersoldiers the basics of how computer networks work and interact, preparing them for more advanced college courses.

databases, computer graphics, and concurrency theory—the concepts behind systems in which several computations are taking place at once and possibly interacting with each other. They also teach computer programming, but not as a central focus of study.

Other computer science programs emphasize advanced programming over theory. These programs, found at four-year colleges, two-year technical and vocational schools, and even some high schools, focus on the skills needed for those wanting to enter the software industry. This aspect of computer science is often referred to as software engineering.

Qualifications for entering a computer science program vary among schools. Applicants will most likely need a high school diploma or GED and will have to complete the college application process, including any required standardized testing. Some computer science majors can start out by taking introductory courses at their college, but it is a good idea to have a firm grasp of computing basics before leaving high school. Introductory classes in computer theory and programming are offered at many high schools. Potential computer science majors will also need a strong background and interest in mathematics and will likely be required to take highly advanced math classes.

INFORMATION TECHNOLOGY

Information technology encompasses the study, design, development, implementation, support, or management of computer-based information systems, particularly computer hardware and software applications. The field deals with using computers and software to convert, process, transmit, store, protect, and retrieve information. Work in the field ranges from installing applications to designing networks and databases. Duties for information technology professionals may include database and software design, hardware engineering, networking, data management, and the management and administration of entire systems.

Recent technological advances have taken the information technology field further away from conventional computers and network technology. Demand is increasing for the ability to integrate technology such as cell phones, personal data assistants, laptop computers, and even televisions. An understanding of how these technologies are integrated can be extremely useful in cyber warfare against terrorist groups that use mobile devices to communicate.

Information technology programs are widely available at four-year colleges and two-year technical schools, though some programs are built into a general computer science program. Background skills and knowledge are similar to those needed for computer science.

Hackers participate in a computer attack and defense competition in Malaysia. Such events bring hackers and network security specialists together to discuss current attack and defense methods.

COMPUTER ENGINEERING

Computer engineering is a discipline that combines computer science with electrical engineering. Computer engineers are usually trained in electrical engineering, software design, and hardware and software integration. They are involved in many aspects of computing, from designing microprocessors, personal computers, and supercomputers to circuit design. Computer engineers are concerned with how computers work and how they are integrated into networks and systems.

Computer engineers need a strong background in science and mathematics, as well as knowledge of electrical engineering. Four-year and postgraduate-level computer engineering programs can be found at major universities with strong engineering schools and computer science programs.

PRIVATE CAREERS

In recent years, private defense-oriented companies and contractors that provide weapons and support for the government have begun hiring cybersoldiers. Companies that have begun recruiting include Northrop Grumman, General Dynamics, Lockheed Martin, and Raytheon. These companies already have major cyber defense contracts with the government and have been at the forefront of research on cyber warfare. As with manufacturing conventional weapons and military equipment, the companies bid against each other for cyber warfare contracts. Several private defense companies have even come together to build a model version of the Internet called the National Cyber Range, which will be used as a digital testing ground for cyber weapons and techniques.

THE GOOGLE ATTACKS

In January 2010, the technology company Google revealed that its computer systems had been subjected to numerous attacks that the company believed originated in China. According to Google, the attacks were aimed at its Gmail e-mail user accounts, including those of Chinese human rights activists and at least thirty-four companies or entities based mostly in California. The company, which had agreed to censor results pulled up by its search engine at the request of the Chinese government before it was allowed to operate in China, threatened to pull out of the country. The company later traced the origin of the attacks to two Chinese schools.

Private defense companies look for several kinds of specialists for their cyber warfare operations. Career paths at these companies include kernel developers, who build the central components of computer operating systems; reverse engineers, who deconstruct programs and hardware devices to determine how they were put together and to find weaknesses; and vulnerability and intrusion detection engineers, who can set up security systems and find ways to exploit existing systems.

Other positions are open to people with experience in intelligence and information systems, as well as media sanitization specialists, who are knowledgeable about methods for clearing data from computer hardware and data storage devices.

CYBER WARFARE, PRESENT AND FUTURE

Network security systems and specialists have the task of defending against cyber attacks as they happen. Security measures include user authentication passwords, firewalls, and antivirus software and intrusion prevention systems that are designed to detect and inhibit malware and trojan horse programs. Encryption makes it more difficult to intercept and interpret information sent over a network. Programs called honeypots serve as decoy network-accessible resources

Secretary of State Hillary Rodham Clinton calls for a probe of the Chinese cyber attack on Google during a January 2010 speech on Internet freedom.

used as detection and early-warning tools. Businesses and governments needing extra security multiply these measures, restrict access to their networks to trusted users, and even isolate a network from other networks as a way to cut off attackers.

Network security specialists can be a great asset to cybersoldiers. After a cyber attack, security specialists often examine the methods used by the attackers in order to gain insight into how the attack was carried out and prevent future attacks. In the case of military and government network security, the information uncovered by security specialists often gets passed on to cybersoldiers, who can put it to use in their own field.

On a large scale, the government's Defense Advanced Research Projects Agency (DARPA) is actively working to track the origins of cyber attacks through a four-year, $43 million effort called the Cyber Genome Project. The agency's goal for the project is to use digital artifacts collected from computer systems, networks, and storage devices to create new techniques for cyber defense and investigations. Specifically, DARPA is conducting technical research in the field of cyber genetics to chart the origins and understand the evolution of digital artifacts such as malware and software. Other research areas include cyber anthropology and sociology, which aim to investigate the social relationships between artifacts and the interactions between software and its users. The program also studies cyber physiology, which involves developing technologies that can automatically analyze software to help researchers understand its function and intent.

PREEMPTIVE STRIKES

Some network security experts, however, believe that DARPA's approach of gathering information from previous attacks handicaps efforts to end cyberterrorist strikes against the country's networks. They argue that cyberterrorists have become too skilled at getting around new security measures and evading detection. These experts feel the best way to defend against cyber attacks is for the government to aggressively use cyber warfare techniques against networks used by cyberterrorists.

However, DARPA's forensic approach to combating cyberterrorism has many supporters. They argue that the Cyber Genome Project and similar operations will help trace the sources of attacks and even enable the United States to launch cyber attacks against them. In January 2010, Secretary of State Hillary Rodham Clinton gave a speech in which she said that cyberattacks against the United States would not be ignored. Clinton stopped short of stating how the United States would respond, other than the possibility that countries that knowingly launch cyberattacks could suffer damage to their reputations and face financial repercussions. If the United States has established an official policy on preemptive cyberattacks, it has not yet been made public. The NSA's use of cyber warfare in taking control of insurgent communications in Iraq in 2007 indicates that the government may be willing to launch its own cyberattacks.

circumvent To avoid or get around, often through cleverness and wit.

computer forensics A science involving the recovery of evidence found in computers.

cyberspace The realm of electronic communication.

cyber warfare An assault on electronic communication networks.

espionage The act or practice of spying.

exploit To use or manipulate to one's advantage.

firewall A collection of security measures designed to prevent unauthorized electronic access to a networked computer system.

hacker A computer user who seeks to gain unauthorized access to computer networks or files.

hardware The mechanical, magnetic, electronic, and electrical components that make up a computer system.

infrastructure The basic facilities, services, and installations needed for the functioning of a community or society.

logistics The planning, implementation, and coordination of the details of a business or other operation.

malware Malicious computer software that interferes with normal computer functions or sends personal data about the user to unauthorized parties over the Internet.

network An interconnected system containing computers and other electronic equipment used for communication.

preempt To prevent by acting first.

propaganda Information, ideas, or rumors deliberately spread widely to help or harm a person, group, movement, institution, or nation.

protocols A set of rules governing the format of messages that are exchanged between computers.

reverse engineer To study or analyze a device to learn details of design, construction, and operation.

software Programs used to direct a computer.

terrorism The use of violence and threats to intimidate and coerce.

trojan horse A computer program planted illegally in another program to do damage locally when the software is activated.

Air Force Institute of Technology
2950 Hobson Way
WPAFB, OH 45433
Web site: http://www.afit.edu
(937) 255-3636
The Air Force Institute of Technology is the air force's
    school of technology and management.

Canadian Cyber Incident Response Centre (CCIRC)
269 Laurier Avenue West
Ottawa, ON K1A 0P8
Canada
(613) 944-4875
Web site: http://www.publicsafety.gc.ca/prg/em/ccirc/
    index-eng.aspx
The CCIRC is responsible for monitoring threats and coor-
    dinating the national response to any cyber security
    incident.

Canadian Security Association
610 Alden Road, Suite 100
Markham, ON L3R 9Z1
Canada
(905) 513-0622
Web site: http://www.canasa.org
The Canadian Security Association is a national nonprofit
    organization dedicated to promoting the safety and secu-
    rity of Canadians.

Central Intelligence Agency (CIA)
Office of Public Affairs
Washington, DC 20505
(703) 482-0623
Web site: https://www.cia.gov
The CIA is among the highest law enforcement bodies in
the United States.

Computer History Museum
1401 N. Shoreline Boulevard
Mountain View, CA 94043
(650) 810-1010
Web site: http://www.computerhistory.org
The Computer History Museum is dedicated to celebrating
computer history.

Federal Bureau of Investigation (FBI)
J. Edgar Hoover Building
935 Pennsylvania Avenue NW
Washington, DC 20535-0001
(202) 324-3000
Web site: http://www.fbi.gov
The FBI's priorities include national security and investigat-
ing federal crimes.

2600: The Hacker Quarterly
P.O. Box 752
Middle Island, NY 11953
(631) 751-2600
Web site: http://www.2600.com

2600 is a magazine for computer hackers and those who
want to learn how to prevent hacking. It was founded
in 1987.

U.S. Department of Defense
1400 Defense Pentagon
Washington, DC 20301-1400
(703) 571-3343
Web site: http://www.defense.gov
The Defense Department oversees the branches of the
military.

WEB SITES

Due to the changing nature of Internet links, Rosen
Publishing has developed an online list of Web sites related
to the subject of this book. This site is updated regularly.
Please use this link to access the list:

http://www.rosenlinks.com/cict/cce

For Further Reading

Bailey, Diane. *Cyber Ethics.* New York, NY: Rosen Publishing Group, 2008.

Campbell, Geoffrey. *A Vulnerable America: An Overview of National Security.* Farmington Hills, MI: Lucent Books, 2004.

Doctorow, Cory. *Little Brother.* New York, NY: Tor Teen, 2008.

Fridell, Ron. *Privacy vs. Security: Your Rights in Conflict.* Berkley Heights, NJ: Enslow Publishers, 2004.

Gerdes, Louise I., ed. *Cyber Crime.* Farmington Hills, MI: Greenhaven Press, 2009.

Hanes, Richard, and Sharon Hanes. *Crime and Punishment in America.* Detroit, MI: UXL, 2005.

Hansen, Paul. *Operations Officer: And Careers in the CIA.* Berkley Heights, NJ: Enslow Publishers, 2006.

Jinks, Catherine. *Evil Genius.* Orlando, FL: Harcourt, 2005.

Katz, Samuel M. *U.S. Counterstrike: American Terrorism.* Minneapolis, MN: Lerner Publications, 2005.

Koestler-Grack, Rachel A. *The Department of Homeland Security.* New York, NY: Chelsea House, 2007.

Miller, Debra, ed. *Espionage and Intelligence.* Farmington Hills, MI: Greenhaven Press, 2007.

Parks, Peggy J. *Computer Hacking* (Crime Scene Investigations). Farmington Hills, MI: Lucent Books, 2008.

Sherman, Josepha. *Charles Babbage and the Story of the First Computer.* Newark, DE: Mitchell Lane Publishers, 2005.

Bain, Ben. "DARPA: Calling All Cybergeneticists."
    Federal Computer Week, January 29, 2010.
    Retrieved February 25, 2010 (http://fcw.com/
    articles/2010/01/29/web-darpa-cyber-genome.
    aspx?sc_lang=en).

Baldor, Lolita C. "Obama Announces U.S. Cyber Security
    Plan." MSNBC, May 29, 2009. Retrieved February 25,
    2010 (http://www.msnbc.msn.com/id/30998004).

Ballard, Mark. "Military Seeks Private Sector Help to
    Build Cyber Warfare Capability." *Computer Weekly*,
    January 29, 2010. Retrieved February 25, 2010
    (http://www.computerweekly.com/Articles/2010/02/
    18/240120/Military-seeks-private-sector-help-to-build-
    cyber-warfare.htm).

Berntsen, Gary. *Human Intelligence, Counterterrorism, and
    National Leadership: A Practical Guide.* Washington, DC:
    Potomac Books, 2008.

Branigan, Steven. *High-Tech Crimes Revealed: Cyberwar Stories
    from the Digital Front.* Boston, MA: Addison-Wesley, 2005.

Christian Science Monitor. "Obama's Smart Pick for
    Cyber Czar: Howard Schmidt." December 23, 2009.
    Retrieved February 25, 2010 (http://www.csmonitor.
    com/Commentary/the-monitors-view/2009/1223/
    Obama-s-smart-pick-for-cyber-czar-Howard-Schmidt).

Corrin, Amber. "Navy Commissions Cyber Defense
    Command." *Defense Systems*, January 29, 2010. Retrieved
    February 25, 2010 (http://www.defensesystems.com/
    Articles/2010/01/29/Navy-cyber-command.aspx).

Halpin, Edward, ed. *Cyberwar, Netwar, and the Revolution in Military Affairs.* New York, NY: Palgrave Macmillan, 2006.

Harris, Shane. "The Cyberwar Plan." *National Journal Magazine,* November 14, 2009. Retrieved February 25, 2010 (http://www.nationaljournal.com/njmagazine/cs_20091114_3145.php).

Jacobs, Andrew, and Miguel Helft. "Google, Citing Cyber Attacks, Threatens to Exit China." *New York Times,* January 12, 2010. Retrieved February 25, 2010 (http://www.nytimes.com/2010/01/13/world/asia/13beijing.html).

Lander, Mark, and John Markoff. "Digital Fears Emerge After Data Siege in Estonia." *New York Times,* May 29, 2007. Retrieved February 25, 2010 (http://www.nytimes.com/2007/05/29/technology/29estonia.html?_r=1).

Lopez, C. Todd. "Fighting in Cyberspace Means Cyber Domain Dominance." *Air Force Print News,* February 28, 2007. Retrieved February 25, 2010 (http://www.af.mil/news/story.asp?id=123042670).

Milburn, John. "Army Crafts Blueprint for Cyber Warfare." *Army Times,* September 10, 2009. Retrieved February 25, 2010 (http://www.armytimes.com/news/2009/09/ap_army_cyberwarfare_091009).

Mitnick, Kevin. *The Art of Intrusion: The Real Stories Behind the Exploits of Hackers, Intruders, and Deceivers.* Indianapolis, IN: Wiley Publishing, 2005.

Munro, Neil. "Cyber Warriors." *Government Executive,* October 29, 2007. Retrieved February 25, 2010

(http://www.govexec.com/story_page.cfm?filepath=/
dailyfed/1007/102907ol.htm).

Nakashima, Ellen. "Gen. Keith Alexander Confirmed to
Head Cyber-Command." *Washington Post,* May 11, 2010.
Retrieved May 14, 2010 (http://www.washington
post.com/wp-dyn/content/article/2010/05/10/
AR2010051005251.html).

Perrow, Charles. *The Next Catastrophe: Reducing Our
Vulnerabilities to Natural, Industrial, and Terrorist Disasters.*
Princeton, NJ: Princeton University Press, 2007.

Posner, Gerald. "China's Secret Cyberterrorism." *Daily Beast,*
January 13, 2010. Retrieved February 25, 2010 (http://
www.thedailybeast.com/blogs-and-stories/2010-01-13/
chinas-secret-cyber-terrorism/p).

Sageman, Marc. *Leaderless Jihad: Terror Networks in the Twenty-
First Century.* Philadelphia, PA: University of Pennsylvania
Press, 2008.

Sanger, David E. "In Digital Combat, U.S. Finds No Easy
Deterrent." *Honolulu Star-Bulletin,* January 10, 2010.
Retrieved February 25, 2010 (http://www.starbulletin.
com/news/nyt/20100126_In_digital_combat_US_finds_
no_easy_deterrent.html).

Schactman, Noah. "Air Force Suspends Controversial
Cyber Command." *Wired,* August 13, 2008. Retrieved
February 25, 2010 (http://www.wired.com/
dangerroom/2008/08/air-force-suspe).

Shanker, Thom. "Cyberwar Nominee Sees Gaps in Law."
New York Times, April 14, 2010. Retrieved May 14,
2010. (http://www.nytimes.com/2010/04/15/
world/15military.html).

Strickland, Aaron. "Navy Cyber Forces Established." Navy.mil, January 26, 2010. Retrieved February 25, 2010 (http://www.navy.mil/search/display.asp?story_id=50853).

Thompson, Mark. "U.S. Pentagon Cyberwar Strategy: The Pentagon Plans to Attack." *Time*, February 2, 2010. Retrieved February 25, 2010 (http://www.time.com/time/nation/article/0,8599,1957679,00.html).

Weimann, Gabriel. *Terror on the Internet: The New Arena, the New Challenges.* Washington, DC: United States Institute of Peace Press, 2006.

ABOUT THE AUTHOR

Jason Porterfield is a writer and journalist living in Chicago. He has written more than twenty books for Rosen Publishing on topics including digital information and digital literacy.

PHOTO CREDITS

Cover (background, front and back), p. 1 © www.istockphoto.com/Andrey Prokhorov; cover (front inset) Tech. Sgt. Cecilio Ricardo/U.S. Air Force; pp. 7, 46 © AP Images; p. 9 © Ints Kalnins/Reuters/Landov; p. 12 White House Photograph; pp. 16, 20 AFP/Getty Images; p. 18 Francois Guillot/AFP/Getty Images; p. 27 Air Force Master Sgt. Adam M. Stump/Department of Defense; p. 29 Capt. Carrie Kessler/U.S. Air Force; p. 31 Rick Naystatt/U.S. Navy; p. 33 Mass Communication Specialist 3rd Class Michael A. Lantron/U.S. Navy; p. 42 Issouf Sanogo/AFP/Getty Images; p. 45 www.jsf.mil; p. 56 FBI; p. 59 © Bob Daemmrich/The Image Works; p. 61 © Bazuki Muhammad/Reuters/Landov; p. 64 Andrew Harrer/Bloomberg/Getty Images.

Designer: Matthew Cauli; Editor: Nicholas Croce; Photo Researcher: Amy Feinberg